Selling Ottumwa

Advertisements
1880 to 1970

Leigh Michaels
Michael W. Lemberger

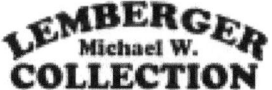

PBL Limited
Ottumwa Iowa

This edition published 2013

10 9 8 7 6 5 4 3 2 1

ISBN 1892689502
ISBN 13: 9781892689504

Printed in the United States of America

Illustrations courtesy of **The Lemberger Collection**. For more information about the collection, which has been called the largest and best-documented privately-owned photography collection in the world, visit www.mlemberger.com.

Visit our website at www.pbllimited.com for more information about this and other publications. Quantity and wholesale prices are available.

Selling Ottumwa

Advertisements
1880 to 1970

Selling Ottumwa

Holland's City Directory 1882

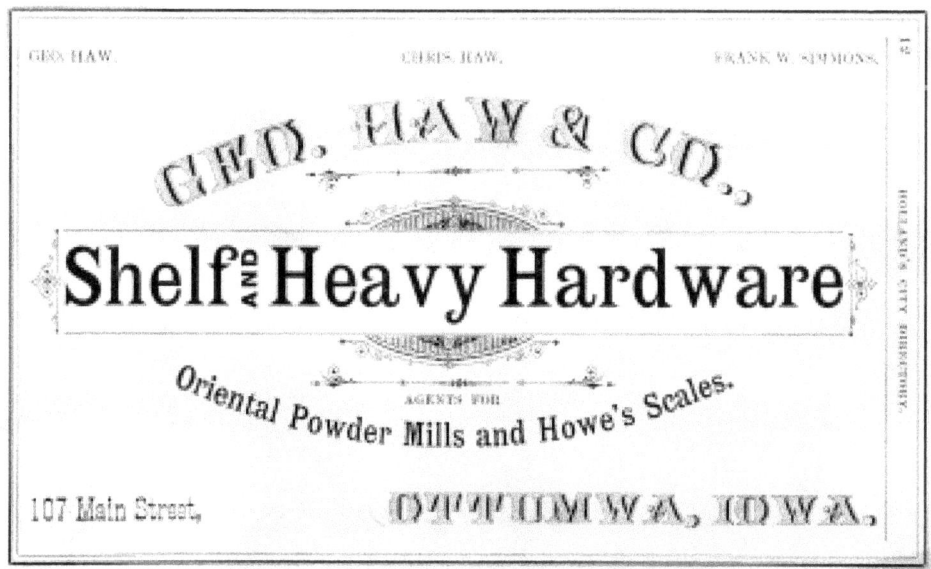

Holland's City Directory 1882

About this Book

Since the days of Pompeii (and probably long before the volcanic eruption of Mount Vesuvius in 79 AD buried that city with many of its ads intact), businesses have advertised their wares, their services, their staffs and owners, and their locations.

Years later, those ads serve as a time capsule. Ads show how commerce has changed through the years. Following ads through succeeding decades shows how a business developed -- when it moved or grew, what its specialties were, who was in charge.

Many of the ads reproduced in this book were originally published in directories which listed all residents and businesses in Ottumwa, Iowa, during a particular year. In choosing ads to include, we have focused on locally-owned businesses. The date and source of the ad is listed below each illustration.

Where possible, ads have been restored, but because of the age of the source material, some damage could not be repaired. Some directories are stained, and a few display additions -- extra notes, calculations, or scribbles on the pages.

We hope you will enjoy visiting Ottumwa's past through the adverting campaigns of the city's industries and businesses.

Holland's City Directory 1882

Holland's City Directory 1882

ARTHUR GEPHART,

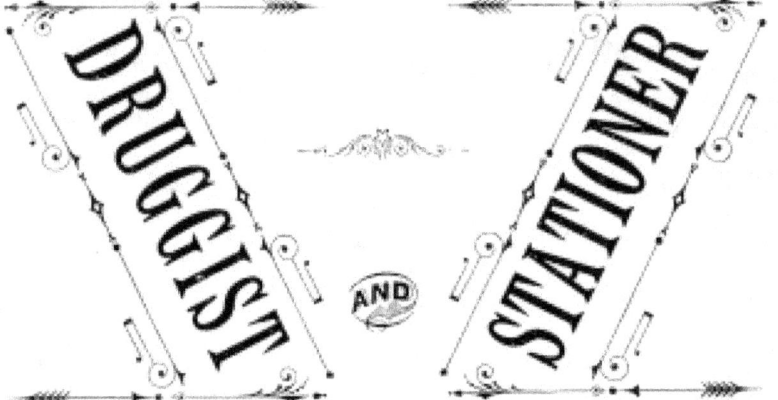

→Toilet and Fancy Articles←

206 East Main Street,

OTTUMWA. IOWA.

Physicians Prescriptions Carefully Dispensed.

Holland's City Directory 1882

Ads from 1880 to 1970

Holland's City Directory 1882

"ISRAEL

THE

HATTER"

AND

GENT'S FURNISHER.

COURT STREET.

KRANER, HOFMANN & CO.,

BREWERS AND MALTSTERS

312 to 320 West Main Street,

OTTUMWA, IOWA.

Holland's City Directory 1882

D. B. WALLACE,

DEALER IN

Fine Guns
AMMUNITION
Revolvers
Sporting
Goods.

Seins, Nets
and
Fishing
Tackle.
All Kinds

Agent Hazard Powder Company.

326 East Main Street,

OTTUMWA, IOWA.

ORDERS FILLED ON SHORT NOTICE.

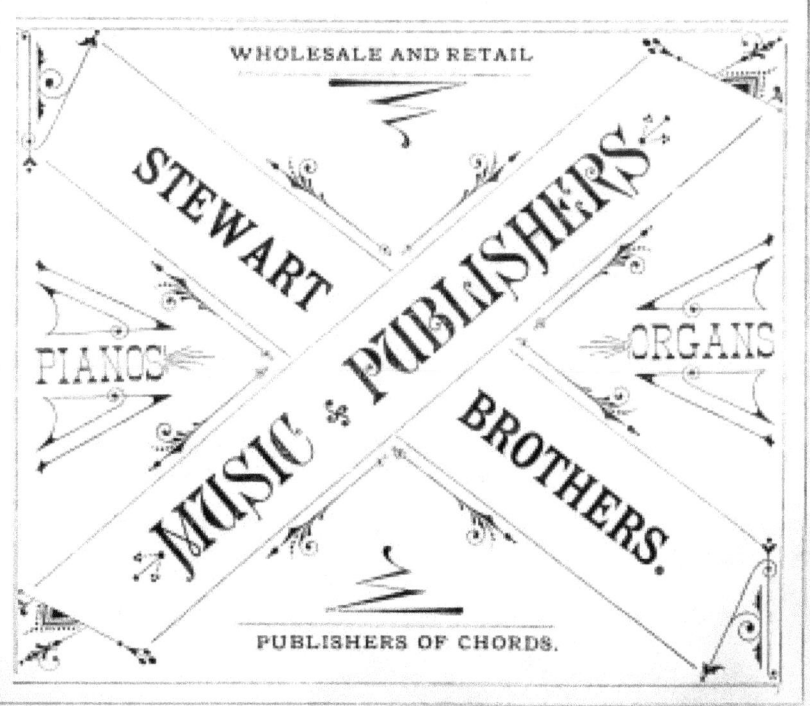

WHOLESALE AND RETAIL

STEWART

PUBLISHERS

PIANOS

ORGANS

MUSIC & PUBLISHERS

BROTHERS.

PUBLISHERS OF CHORDS.

Holland's City Directory 1882

McINTOSH & CO.,

Commission Merchants,

Butter, Eggs, Fruit, Poultry,

Hides, Tallow, etc.

REFERNCES { Iowa National Bank, } OTTUMWA.
{ Lilburn, Baker & Co. }

109 MARKET STREET.

CHAS. A. WALSH,

ATTORNEY AT LAW,

—AND—

STENOGRAPHER.

Office at Court House.

Holland's City Directory 1882

Ads from 1880 to 1970

⇒OTTUMWA⇐

DAILY + AND + WEEKLY

"COURIER"

The Daily is Published every Evening, and the
Weekly on Wednesday Morning. The Daily
is an Eight Column Paper, and has the
Largest Circulation of any Daily in
the Sixth Congressional District.

Price per annum, - $7.00,
"   per quarter, - $1.75.

The Weekly was Established in 1848, and has
been Published Continuously ever since. It
is a Ten Column Paper, and as Large
as any Weekly in the State.

Price, $1.50 per year, in advance.

It is the Best Advertising Medium in
Southern Iowa.

The Largest and Best Job Office in the City connected with the Paper.

A. H. HAMILTON, PROPRIETOR.

Holland's City Directory 1882

13

Holland's City Directory 1882

Holland's City Directory 1882

Holland's City Directory 1882

Holland's City Directory 1882

CHAS. REIFSNYDER,

DEALER IN

Fresh and Salt Meats

OF ALL KINDS,

Fish, Oysters, Vegetables, Butter and Eggs,

No. 516 East Main Street.

J. M. LAMME,

PROPRIETOR

WAPELLO MILLS,

DEALER IN

Flour, Grain, Meal, Chop Feed, &c.

OTTUMWA, IOWA.

AUGUSTUS ILSE

RESTAURANT

Boarding by Day or Week at Most Reasonable Rates.

Best Bath Rooms in the City, in Connection.

504 EAST MAIN.

J. T. McCUNE,

BAKER, CONFECTIONER,

AND DEALER IN

STAPLE AND FANCY GROCERIES,

Corner Main and College Streets.

Holland's City Directory 1882

Holland's City Directory 1882

Holland's City Directory 1882

Take The Ballingall Bus on your arrival.

MANCHESTER & CARTER.

Holland's City Directory 1882

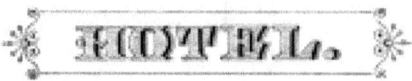

ENGLISH KITCHEN
HOTEL.

MRS. D. HODGE, - - - Proprietor.

This New Hotel is First Class in all its Appointments.
Centrally Located. Convenient Sample Rooms.
Good Billiard Hall, &c.

'BUS TO AND FROM ALL TRAINS.

OYSTERS A LA RESTAURANT, IN THEIR SEASON.

DOORS NEVER CLOSED

THE BEST.   STOP THERE.

LOUIS SCHAUB,

General Teamster.

—ALL KINDS OF—

TRANSFERRING DONE.

Holland's City Directory 1882

Ads from 1880 to 1970

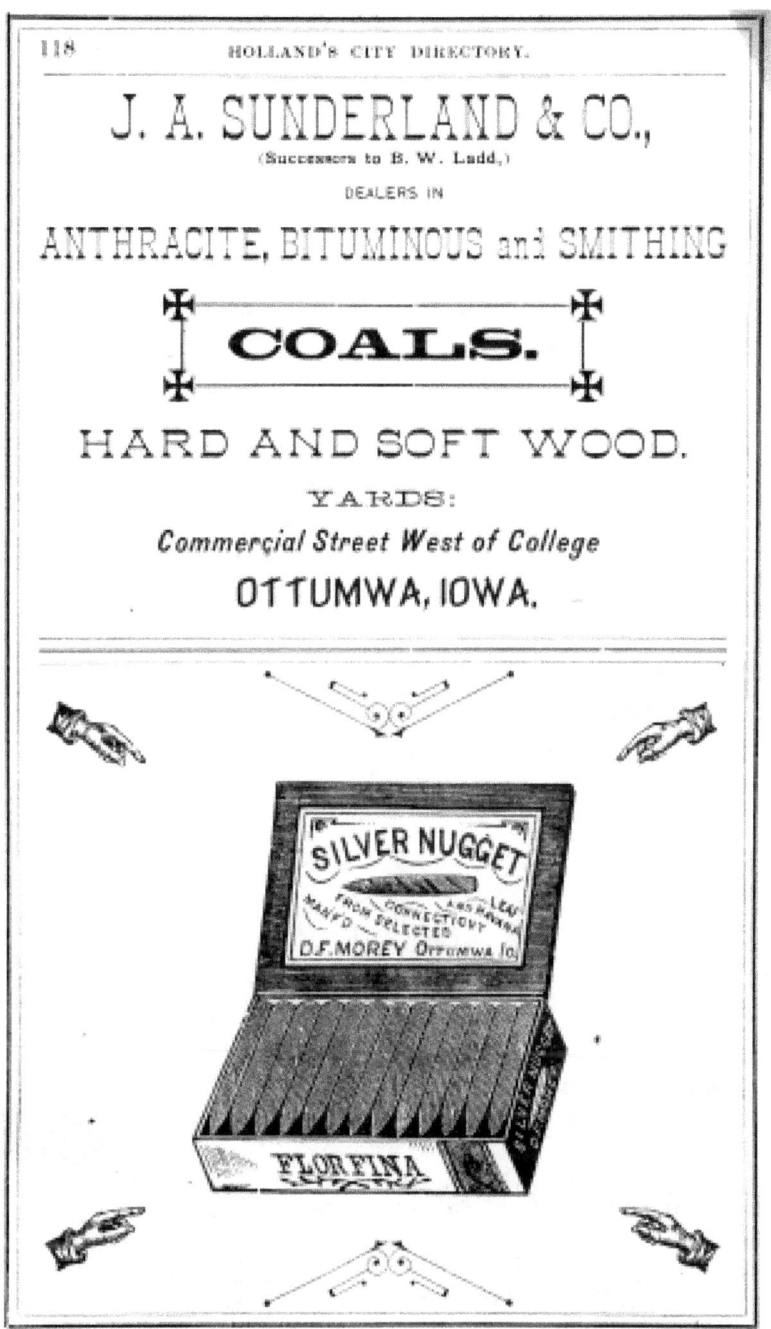

Holland's City Directory 1882

Holland's City Directory 1882

24

Ads from 1880 to 1970

Holland's City Directory 1882

N. P. WIND & CO.,

WHOLESALE

WINES AND LIQUORS,

116 Whiting Block, Second Street,

OTTUMWA, IOWA.

FRED SWENSON

MERCHANT TAILOR

330 East Main Street,
OTTUMWA, IOWA.

Holland's City Directory 1882

A. F. BROEGE,

Merchant Tailor,

233 EAST MAIN ST.

OTTUMWA. - - IOWA.

J. H. RHOEM,

DEALER IN

ALL KINDS OF

Musical Merchandise,

PIANOS, ORGANS & SMALL GOODS,

OTTUMWA IOWA.

Holland's City Directory 1882

F. G. RANDALL & CO.,

AND

MANUFACTURERS,

CORNER OF COURT and SECOND STREETS,

OTTUMWA, IOWA.

J. HATCH,

DEALER IN ALL KINDS OF

Ladies' and Gent's Fur Goods.

Also Headquarters for the

"NOBLE SHIRT,"

All Kinds of Underwear.

406 E. Main Street,   3 doors East of Jefferson.

OTTUMWA, IOWA.

Holland's City Directory 1882

Ads from 1880 to 1970

ANDY DUMMLER,

PROPRIETOR

ANDY'S SAMPLE ROOMS

AND BILLIARD HALL.

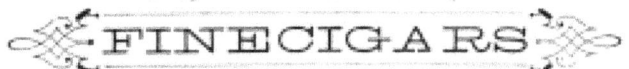

Fine Wines and Liquors a Specialty.

Only the Best Goods Kept.

FINE CIGARS

223 Main St. bet. Market and Green,   OTTUMWA, IOWA.

MAGNOLIA RESTAURANT,

Market St. opp. Corn Exchange.

Lunch & Meals Served at all Hours

DAY OR NIGHT.

Railroad Men Find the Magnolia a Convenient
place to get their Lunch.

J. M. GIBBS & SON, Proprietors,
OTTUMWA, IOWA.

Holland's City Directory 1882

Holland's City Directory 1882

Ads from 1880 to 1970

Holland's City Directory 1882

DIRECTORS:

T. D. FOSTER,	J. T. HACKWORTH,	J. G. HUTCHISON,
J. C. OSGOOD,	CHAS. P. BROWN,	JOS. LOOMIS,
J. C. JORDAN,	DAN'L ZOLLARS,	C. O. TAYLOR.

CAPITAL $100,000

Authorized Capital, $250,000.

CORRESPONDENTS:

National Bank of Illinois, Chicago; Merchants National Bank, Chicago, Fourth National Bank, New York. U. S. National Bank, New York. Merchants National Bank, St. Louis. First National Bank, Burlington.

ACCOUNTS SOLICITED.

Holland's City Directory 1882

Ads from 1880 to 1970

Holland's City Directory 1882

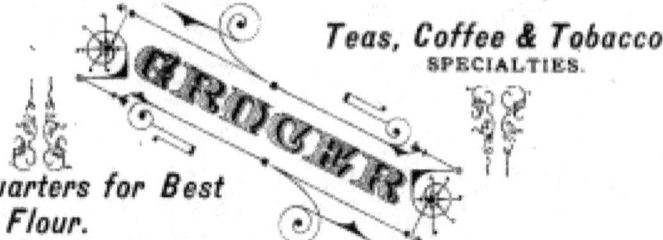

Holland's City Directory 1882

Holland's City Directory 1882

Ottumwa City Directory 1890

Ads from 1880 to 1970

HARNED & SULLIVAN,

(Successors to Workman & Bayliss)

UNDERTAKERS

TELEPHONE 85.

OPEN DAY AND NIGHT.

Burial Robes of every description on hand. Particular Attention given to Embalming.

FINE BLACK HEARSE .... FINE WHITE HEARSE

◁115❖WEST❖SECOND❖STREET▷

NEXT TO FORD'S LIVERY.

OTTUMWA, - - - IOWA.

Ottumwa City Directory 1890

Listen to What We Say

You Can Travel On The Old Reliable

DIAMOND JO LINE
STEAMERS

Cheaper Than You Can Board At A First-Class Resort.

PATRONS OF THE
GREAT RIVER ROUTE

Secure all the Elegance and Comforts of a First-Class Hotel while
seeing the ever changing and

MAGNIFICENT SCENERY OF THE MISSISSIPPI RIVER.

The Steamers of this line are provided with every known convenience for

Safety, Comfort and Speed,

And are commanded by able and experienced officers, and their tables
are supplied with every obtainable luxury.
For Rates and Information apply to

Isaac P. Lusk, General Passenger Agent, St. Louis, Mo.

Ottumwa City Directory 1901

Selling Ottumwa

WYMAN-RAND CARPET CO. AND : : : :
: : : : HALL-EKFELT FURNITURE CO.

Complete House Furnishers. : That's All.

McCoy's Ottumwa City Directory 1903

Ads from 1880 to 1970

McCoy's Ottumwa City Directory 1903

Ottumwa City Directory 1907

Fair-Williams Bridge & Manufacturing Co.

MANUFACTURERS OF

BRIDGES

AND ARCHITECTURAL
IRON WORK

403, 405 and 407 South Vine Street   OTTUMWA, IA.

McCoy's Ottumwa City Directory 1905

Ads from 1880 to 1970

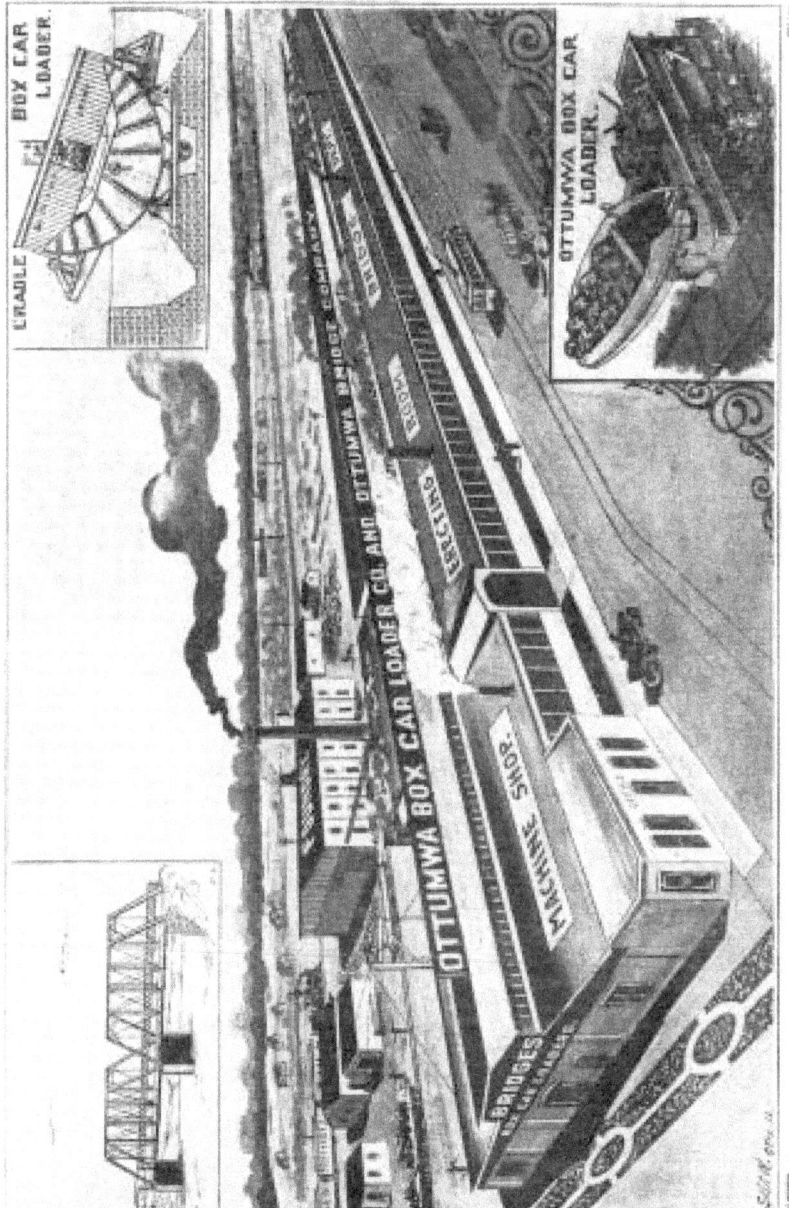

Ottumwa City Directory 1907

Ottumwa Stamp Works

A. G. WALLACE, Proprietor.

THIS BOUQUET IS FOR YOU.

PRINTED WITH THREE IMPRESSIONS ON ONE OF OUR COLTS ARMORY PRESSES.

YES!

WE PRINT ROSES, OR ANYTHING ELSE, FROM A VISITING CARD TO A NEWSPAPER. IF YOU FEEL A LONGING TO SEE HOW COLOR PRINTING, EMBOSSING, COATING, ETC., IS DONE YOU ARE INVITED TO STOP IN AT 215 AND 217 EAST MAIN STREET, WHERE YOU WILL FIND ONE OF THE MOST COMPLETE AND UP-TO-DATE PRINTING PLANTS IN THE STATE, EQUIPPED WITH THE LATEST MODERN MACHINERY AND MATERIAL, NECESSARY FOR THE EXECUTION OF THE PRODUCTS TURNED OUT BY THE

OTTUMWA STAMP WORKS

215-217 East Main Street.

Ottumwa City Directory 1907

Ads from 1880 to 1970

Ottumwa City Directory 1907

Ottumwa Brewing & Ice Co.

OTTUMWA, IOWA

Brewers of the Celebrated Keg and Bottled Beers

Ottumwa Budd
and Bohemian

McCoy's Ottumwa City Directory 1912

Something New Every Day at
The Fashion Center

DONELAN'S

Ottumwa's Biggest, Best and Busiest Store

WE LEAD IN

DRY GOODS

Millinery, Carpets, Shoes, Coats
Suits, Men's Furnishings

The Largest Assortment   Prices Always the Lowest

McCoy's Ottumwa City Directory 1912

The
Ballingall
Ottumwa, Iowa

Newly Remodeled   **Thoroughly Modern**

American Plan

$2, $2.50, $3 and $3.50 Per Day

E. A. MANCHESTER
MANAGER

McCoy's Ottumwa City Directory 1912

Ads from 1880 to 1970

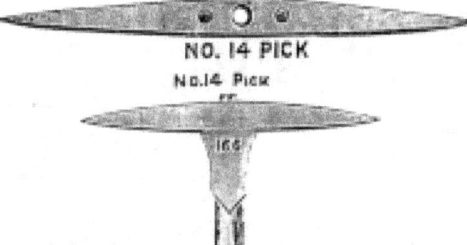
McCoy's Ottumwa City Directory 1912

McCoy's Ottumwa City Directory 1912

 **O K**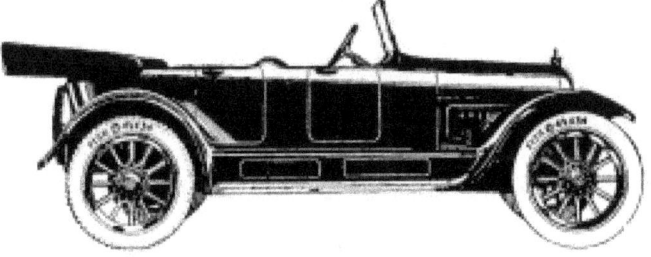

IN EVERY WAY

The Cars With the Five Essentials

APPEARANCE - PERFORMANCE - COMFORT - SERVICE - PRICE

On Display at

OVERLAND OTTUMWA CO.   **Phone 314**

Willard Storage Battery
Service Station

We have the most modern and up-to-date
Service Station in Southeastern Iowa.

Give us a trial and be convinced that we
Excel All.

ELDRIDGE BATTERY CO.

134 W. Second St.   **Ottumwa, Iowa**

Ottumwa City Directory 1918

Ottumwa City Directory 1918

Ads from 1880 to 1970

Ottumwa City Directory 1918

Ottumwa City Directory 1920

CHAS. T. SULLIVAN   LESTER JAY

SULLIVAN & JAY

Undertakers and Licensed Embalmers

EFFICIENT SERVICE
COURTEOUS TREATMENT
MODERN EQUIPMENT

Oldest Undertaking Establishment in city. First class Chapel, Morgue, Parlors and Rest Room in connection. Complete Stock of High Class Funeral Supplies.

Phone 122   130-132 West 2nd St.

DAY OR NIGHT

Ottumwa City Directory 1920

Ottumwa City Directory 1920

Ottumwa City Directory 1935

PROFESSIONAL BLUE BOOK

PHYSICIANS AND SURGEONS

H. W. SELLERS, M. D.

GENITO-URINARY DISEASES

MEDICAL GYNECOLOGY

Phone 1481   309 E. Main St.

H. A. SPILMAN
X-RAY AND SURGERY

S. A. SPILMAN
SURGERY AND
CONSULTATION

26 Hofmann Block   Phone 377

Ottumwa City Directory 1935

Ottumwa City Directory 1935

Ads from 1880 to 1970

Ottumwa City Directory 1935

Ottumwa City Directory 1935

Ads from 1880 to 1970

Ottumwa City Directory 1935

DEPARTMENT STORES

Ottumwa City Directory 1935

Ottumwa City Directory 1935

Ads from 1880 to 1970

Samuel Mahon Company

WHOLESALE GROCERS — COFFEE ROASTERS

OTTUMWA, IOWA

Creston, Iowa   Ft. Madison, Iowa

PHONE—284—285

HARDWARE

HARPER & McINTIRE CO.

HARDWARE

Sporting Goods, Household Electric Appliances, Roofers and Roofers' Supplies, Stoves, Furnaces and Sheet Metal Work

RETAIL
105 E. Main St.
Phone 17

WHOLESALE
216-218-220-222
Commercial St.

THE PLACE TO GET DATA ON BUSINESSES, PEOPLE AND PLACES IS FROM THE LATEST

City Directory

A VAST WEALTH OF VALUABLE INFORMATION IS ALWAYS AT HAND

Ottumwa City Directory 1935

Ottumwa City Directory 1935

Ads from 1880 to 1970

Ottumwa City Directory 1935

PASTEURIZED
DAIRY PRODUCTS

Photo by Van's Studio

MILK

Cream - Buttermilk - Orangeade
Butter - Chocolate Milk -
Cottage Cheese

VANDELLO
MILK COMPANY

Phone 674

1107 EAST MAIN ST.   OTTUMWA, IOWA

Ottumwa City Directory 1937

Ottumwa City Directory 1937

DAIRY PRODUCTS

SAFE
PASTEURIZED MILK

Golden Rod Butter – Bireley's Orangeade
Buttermilk – Cottage Cheese – Cream – Cheese

ICE CREAM

Photo by Van's Studio

Phone 801

GRAHAM MILK
COMPANY

627 WEST 2ND ST.   OTTUMWA, IOWA

Ottumwa City Directory 1937

C. M. Henderson Motor Co.

"The Car of the Future"

LINCOLN ZEPHYR. 1937

Phone 636

224 W. 2nd St.

PBL Ltd.

Ottumwa City Directory 1937

Ottumwa City Directory 1951

Ottumwa City Directory 1951

REEVES
AUTO COMPANY

PACKARD

Sales and Service

CASE
Farm Implements

PHONE 1272

207-209 WEST SECOND

"Same Location — Same Make of Cars Since 1910"

(J. H. HARTER, Owner)

Ottumwa City Directory 1951

Ottumwa City Directory 1951

CALL
3300

DELUXE CAB CO.
TAXI

Checker Cab
COMPANY

CALL
177

Featuring "TWO-WAY RADIO" Service
Insuring Prompt Pick-Up — Passenger Insured

114 SOUTH GREEN

Ottumwa City Directory 1951

Ottumwa City Directory 1951

Ads from 1880 to 1970

AIRCRAFT

Ottumwa City Directory 1951

Ottumwa City Directory 1951

McGEE

PLUMBING & HEATING

Complete Installation and Repair Service

 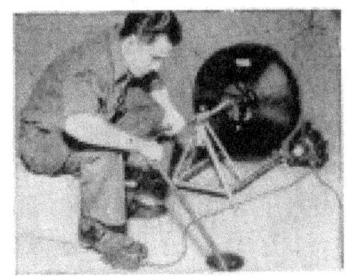

MODERN PLUMBING

*Dependable
Service*

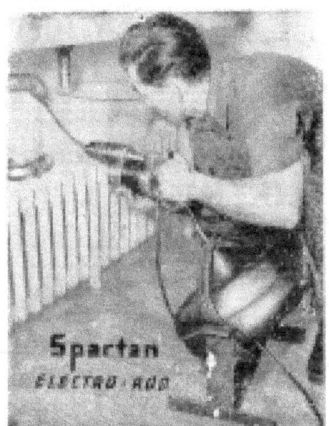

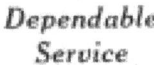

*Prompt
Service*

HOT WATER and STEAM HEATING SYSTEMS
108 N. COURT
DAY OR NIGHT
PHONE 5092

Ottumwa City Directory 1951

Ottumwa City Directory 1955

Ads from 1880 to 1970

Ottumwa City Directory 1955

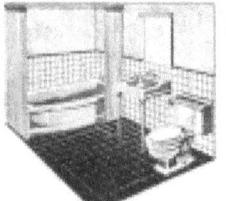  
Ottumwa City Directory 1955

Ads from 1880 to 1970

KEN LAZENBY
REALTOR

TO BUY OR SELL
INSURANCE

TO BUY OR SELL
LOANS

PROPERTY MANAGEMENT — SALES — LEASES — INSURANCE

714 CHURCH ST.   PHONE MUrray 4-6251

RESIDENCE
FARMS

RALPH N. BAKER

INDUSTRIAL
BUSINESS

REAL ESTATE
BROKERS

116 E. 2d   Tel. MUrray 2-5439

GLENN HAZEN REAL ESTATE and INSURANCE

City Homes
Business Property
Farm Lands — Loans
and General Insurance

104 S. Court   Phone MUrray 4-4679   After Hours Phone MUrray 2-0860

Ottumwa City Directory 1955

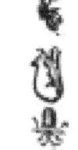

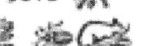

Ottumwa City Directory 1955

Ads from 1880 to 1970

PATTERSON MONUMENT CO.

M. C. PATTERSON — W. E. PATTERSON

Monuments
and
Markers

Portable Machinery for
Cemetery Work

32 Years in Ottumwa

801 Church - Tels. MUrray 2-3176 — 2-0560 — 2-3328

NEWSPAPERS

READ and USE

Courier Classified Ads

You can buy through these columns to an advantage and also, you
can sell or rent through these same columns because
many people read "CLASSIFIED"
ADS every day.

●

PHONE MURRAY 4-4611-2-3

Ottumwa City Directory 1955

PHONE MURRAY 4-4664

Safe – Dependable

2 WAY RADIO DISPATCHED CABS

ANYWHERE   ANY TIME

WELDING

OTTUMWA WELDING CO.

STEEL FABRICATION   ●   AUTOMATIC
HARD SURFACING   ●   PORTABLE WELDING
ORNAMENTAL IRON WORK
LINCOLN and VICTOR WELDING SUPPLIES

416 West Main St.   Dial MUrray 2-5893

WELDING SUPPLIES

619 Church   Tel. MUrray 2-6739

Ottumwa City Directory 1955

Ads from 1880 to 1970

Bud REUSCH PONTIAC

Pontiac

Sales and Service

24 HOUR WRECKER SERVICE

NIGHT PHONE ENTERPRISE 3000

658 W. 2d   Phone MUrray 4-6514

"SWEDE" WATTS Standard Service

   **MOTOR OILS**      **ATLAS TIRES** 

Batteries   STANDARD   **Accessories**

Church and Sheridan Sts.   Tel. MUrray 2-9271

AUTOMOBILE GARAGES

HINKEL'S GARAGE

REPAIRING ALL MAKES and MODELS

CYLINDER REBORING
BRAKE DRUMS TURNED

DAY and NIGHT TOWING

HEAVIEST IN SOUTH IOWA

234 N. SHERIDAN

AAA

DAY PHONE MUrray 2-0673   NIGHT MUrray 2-9938

Ottumwa City Directory 1955

Ottumwa City Directory 1955

Ads from 1880 to 1970

Ottumwa City Directory 1955

Ottumwa City Directory 1955

Ottumwa City Directory 1955

Ottumwa City Directory 1955

FIDELITY SAVINGS BANK

"The White Bank on the Corner"

FOR ALL YOUR BANKING NEEDS

LOW COST
BANK LOANS

for every purpose

•

Home Loans - Farm Loans
Personal Loans - Automobile Loans
F. H. A. Loans - G. I. Loans

•

```
STANLEY A. HAW..............Chairman of the Board
DONALD M. ROWE...........................President
C. R. COLTON...................Vice-President, Cashier
L. A. SPILMAN......Vice-President-Personal Loan Dept.
```

PHONE MUrray 2-5441 for every banking need

Corner MAIN and MARKET STREETS

Ottumwa City Directory 1955

New Home . . .

UNION BANK
AND TRUST COMPANY

Our new home at Third and Market Streets we hope will be ready to serve you in May, 1956. We are pleased to offer the following new conveniences:

Parking Area for 40 Cars
Two Auto Drive-In Windows
One Walk-up Window
Large Comfortable Lobby
Modern Night Depository
All Banking Services Including Safety
Deposit Vault on Sidewalk Level

Serving Southern Iowa Since 1871

Ottumwa City Directory 1955

DAIRIES

Ottumwa City Directory 1955

Ottumwa City Directory 1955

Ads from 1880 to 1970

MARTIN
MACHINE and ELECTRIC CO.

Rewinding and Repairing All Types Electric Motors and Equipment
We Furnish Service Motors

Maintenance and Repairs on Industrial Control Equipment

NEW MOTOR SALES

ENGINEERING SERVICE

Gates V-Belts - Sheaves - Roller Chain and

Sprockets - Flexible Couplings and Pillow Blocks

Contract and General Machine Work

Industrial Supplies

636-38-40 E. Main St.   Ottumwa, Iowa   MUrray 2-3275

ELECTRICAL

CITY ELECTRIC COMPANY
and HOUSE OF TELEVISION

General Electric Contractors

TV-Refrigeration and Repair of all Automatic Appliances

New Installations
and Repairing for
Commercial - Industrial
Residential - Buildings

Just Call Us

Qualified Workmen

MUrray 2-5421

Television, Refrigerators, Deep Freezes, Electric Ranges

Automatic Washers — Automatic Dryers

PHONE MUrray 2-5421   **709-711 CHURCH**

Ottumwa City Directory 1955

DEPARTMENT STORES

Ottumwa City Directory 1955

Ads from 1880 to 1970

Ottumwa City Directory 1955

 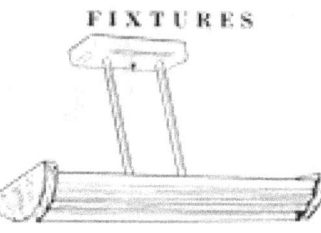
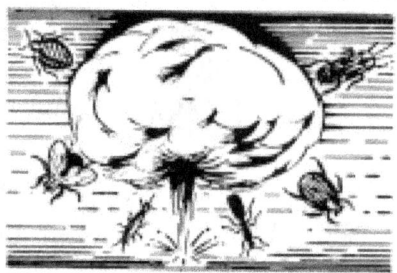

Ottumwa City Directory 1955

Ottumwa City Directory 1955

Ottumwa City Directory 1955

Ads from 1880 to 1970

Ottumwa City Directory 1955

Ottumwa City Directory 1955

Ads from 1880 to 1970

SAM STOLTZ

Department Store
of Insurance

114 E. Third St.   Ottumwa, Ia.   Phone MUrray 2-3528

C. (see) LEO KAPP AGENCY

GENERAL INSURANCE

307 Church St.   Phone MUrray 2-5429

"Don't take the Rap - Insure with KAPP"

OSCAR A. MILLER

Fire and Auto Insurance

UNION BANK BLDG.   TEL. MUrray 2-0325

Ottumwa City Directory 1955

Ottumwa City Directory 1955

106

Ottumwa City Directory 1955

Ottumwa City Directory 1955

Ads from 1880 to 1970

Ottumwa City Directory 1955

HOTELS

INSURANCE

Ottumwa City Directory 1955

Ads from 1880 to 1970

GREEN BAY LUMBER CO.

BUILDING
SUPPLIES
BONDED ROOFING

Quick Delivery of Builders' Supplies

Your Friendly Neighbor

NORTH COURT ROAD   TEL. MURRAY 4-5479

We Have a Complete Stock of High-Grade

Lumber and Building Material

and Will Be Pleased to Quote on Your Requirements

We are equipped to give service that will
meet with your approval.

We will appreciate a portion of your business.

HAWKEYE LUMBER COMPANY

ROY MARINELLI, Manager

647 W. 2d   Phone MUrray 4-6757

Ottumwa City Directory 1955

Ottumwa City Directory 1955

Ads from 1880 to 1970

Ottumwa City Directory 1957

Ottumwa City Directory 1957

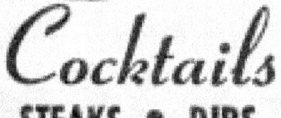

Sylvania Club

EAST ON HWY 34
1 MI EAST OF
CITY LIMITS

DINING
and
DANCING

PIANO BAR

DANCING AFTER
9 PM

Air Conditioned Comfort

*Lovely Atmosphere
Where Friends
Gather For An
Enjoyable Evening*

Cocktails

**STEAKS • RIBS
CHICKEN • SEA FOODS**

PRIME RIB -
SPAGHETTI & MEAT BALLS

*Expertly Prepared -
Perfectly Served*

Open Mon. Through Sat. At 5 P.M.
Closed Sunday

Dial **682-9333**

O T T U M W A

Ottumwa City Directory 1965

Ads from 1880 to 1970

Ottumwa City Directory 1965

Ottumwa City Directory 1965

Ottumwa City Directory 1965

Ads from 1880 to 1970

VARIEL OVERTURF'S

CHUB & WINK'S PIZZA HOUSE

PIZZA!

ORDERS FOR PICK UP
BAKED OR UNBAKED

5 PM - 12 MIDNIGHT
WEEKDAYS & SUNDAY
5 PM - 1 AM FRI. & SAT.
CLOSED MONDAYS

Call 682-9167

512 CHURCH   OTTUMWA

Ottumwa City Directory 1965

HERMAN'S CAFE

COMPLETE
MEALS
SHORT
ORDERS

ORDERS TO GO

OPEN 5:00 AM
TO 8:00 PM

AIR CONDITIONED COMFORT
DANNY RICHARDSON - Owner

CALL 682-9250

321 E MAIN   OTTUMWA

Ottumwa City Directory 1965

Ottumwa City Directory 1965

Ads from 1880 to 1970

Ottumwa City Directory 1970

Selling Ottumwa

NORTHWESTERN BELL TELEPHONE CO.

Find it Fast
In The
Yellow Pages

HOME and BUSINESS EXTENSIONS
TELETYPEWRITER SERVICE

YOUR CUSTOMERS AND OFFICE CAN TYPE ON
THE SAME CONNECTION MAKING
INQUIRY AND IMMEDIATE REPLY POSSIBLE
PROVIDES WRITTEN RECORD
JUST CALL OUR OFFICE

133 N. WASHINGTON ST.   TEL. 682-3411

TELEVISION AND RADIO REPAIRING

PARIS RADIO &

Complete
RADIO and TELEVISION
SERVICE

Tubes for All Makes TV

Pick-Up and Delivery Service

210 S. Union St.   Tel. 682-2020

Television and Radio Sets—Sales and Service

COWLES TV AND APPLIANCE

The Most
Trusted Name
in Television

SALES and SERVICE

TELEVISION
RADIOS—AUTO RADIOS
TAPE RECORDERS
RECORD PLAYERS
ETC.

2849 NORTH COURT RD.   TEL. 684-6509

TIRES—RETREADING

OTTUMWA BANDAG

COLD PROCESS RETREADING FOR TWICE AS MANY MILES AND LONGER LIFE
OF CASINGS - ALL TRUCK AND INDUSTRIAL TIRES - CHOICE OF TREADS
ALL RETREADING DONE IN OTTUMWA

THE WORLD IS BANDAG COUNTRY

637 West Second
Ottumwa

684-4521 OFFICE
684-5004 SHOP

Ottumwa City Directory 1970

Ads from 1880 to 1970

Ottumwa City Directory 1970

For more information about these and other books, calendars and products,
visit
www.pbllimited.com
PBL Limited
P.O. Box 935
Ottumwa Iowa 52501